HIGHER EDUCATION COMPLIANCE

What Governing Boards Really Need to Know

JUDITH W. SPAIN, J.D., CCEP

Higher Education Compliance: What Governing Boards Really Need to Know

Published by MacArthur Publishing House
Judith W. Spain, J. D., CCEP, Author

ISBN: 979-8-218-07156-1
EDUCATION/Administration/Higher

QUANTITY PURCHASES: Schools, companies, professional groups, clubs, and other organizations may qualify for special terms when ordering quantities of this title. For information, email jspain@ higheredcomplianceconsulting.com.

This book is printed in the United States of America.

To my wonderful husband, Norman, who always supports me in all my endeavors.

To our amazing children and spouses, Ben and Allison and Nate and Claire, who are my inspiration.

To our grandchildren, Elin and Leighton, for whom the world is just beginning.

To my Driveway Divas—Karen, Dot, Debbie, Martha, and Julie, who have surrounded me in laughter and friendship for years.

To my walking buddies, Mandy Eppley and Teresa Belluscio, who make sure that I never falter.

To my editors and fellow higher education professionals, Tina Davis, Lisa Macke, Melany Aldridge, Bev Grau, Chip Moore, and Laura Whitaker-Lea, for their assistance in completing this project.

And to all compliance professionals—shoot for the moon!

CONTENTS

CHAPTER 1

ROLE OF BOARD

> We choose to go to the moon. . . . We choose to go to the moon in this decade and do the other things, not because they are easy, but because they are hard; because that goal will serve to organize and measure the best of our energies and skills, because that challenge is one that we are willing to accept, one we are unwilling to postpone, and one we intend to win, and the others, too.[1]
>
> —John F. Kennedy

These are the words from President Kennedy's famous speech delivered on September 12, 1962, at Rice University. It set the tone for the United States' race to the moon.

What did his words *not* say? President Kennedy did not tell the engineers how to design the vehicle to put the United States astronauts on the moon. He did not tell the "human computers" at the National Aeronautics and Space Administration (NASA) how to determine the correct trajectory angles to land on the moon. And he did not tell the metallurgists how to develop new metal alloys when he acknowledged that some of them had "not yet been invented."

What *did* his words say? President Kennedy's words inspired NASA and a host of other agencies, contractors, and employees to develop a plan—a plan to put a man on the moon in that decade. And that goal was achieved. On July 20, 1969, only seven years after President Kennedy's speech, Neil Armstrong stepped on the moon.

This achievement happened because a leader challenged the employees to succeed. This achievement happened because a leader had a vision to adopt and verbalize achievable goals. This achievement happened because a leader had the foresight to understand his role in the governing structure—to provide the vision, the resources, and the support needed by the workers to implement the goal.

As a Board member, you have a vision as well as a fiduciary responsibility to ensure that your institution is in compliance with federal, state, and local laws and regulations as well as with institutional policies. How are you, your Board colleagues, and your institution accomplishing that goal?

Presuming that you are also a member of the business community, you are probably familiar with compliance initiatives for organizations. But have you considered the same type of compliance initiatives at the institution for which you serve on the Board?

It is possible that, at this point, you may not fully understand what you are being challenged to do, so how can you support your institution in a compliance initiative? It is also possible that, based on your leadership role in your non-Board job, you are aware that an entity should have a compliance program, but you do not know what this means in reference to higher education.

This book is designed to walk you through the process—just like NASA built a spaceship. The book begins by explaining the difference between enterprise risk management and compliance risk management and how risk affects institutional decision-making (Chapter 2). Chapter 3 identifies the elements of an effective compliance program using the United States Sentencing Commission Guidelines

(Guidelines), which are the gold standard upon which compliance programs are built.

The next six chapters discuss the development of a compliance risk assessment plan. Chapter 4 discusses the building of a compliance structure. Chapter 5 identifies a possible universe of risk to be assessed. Chapter 6 provides the tools for developing a compliance risk assessment survey. Chapter 6 also describes how to use the factors of likelihood of occurrence and the impact of the occurrence to determine the level of risk to the institution due to noncompliance with a particular law. Once the assessment process is identified and the assessment occurs, the resulting data needs to be evaluated, and a mitigation plan needs to be adopted (Chapter 7). The institution must then develop a process to monitor, reassess, and modify the compliance initiative (Chapter 8). Chapter 9 explains all remaining Guidelines and institutional responsibility for compliance with these Guidelines.

This book approaches all the above issues by providing a comprehensive, step-by-step, scalable method from conception to launch of a compliance initiative for a higher education institution, regardless of whether the institution is public or private, small or large, graduate or undergraduate, technical or trade, and research- or teaching-focused.

The role of the Board is explained clearly in the Guidelines which states:

> *The organization's governing authority shall be knowledgeable about the content and operation of the compliance and ethics program and shall exercise reasonable oversight with respect to the implementation and effectiveness of the compliance and ethics program.* [2]

So before you start into this book, remember your overall role as a Board member. You are not to do the nitty-gritty work necessary to assess compliance with applicable laws and regulations. Rather, you need to challenge your institutional leadership to succeed in implementing an effective ethics and compliance initiative. You need to adopt an appropriate Board Charter that emphasizes the need for this program and verbalizes your achievable goals to the implementers. And you need to understand your role in this process—to provide the vision of what an effective ethics and compliance initiative should be and provide appropriate time and monetary resources to support and encourage the employees who will be working hard to implement the compliance program.

Implementing a compliance initiative will not be easy. Neither was going to the moon, but the United States did it with a coordinated effort of many individuals.

It is a task that your institution and Board can and should accept.

CHAPTER 2

PRIMER ON RISK

CHAPTER GOALS:

- Understand your institutional level of risk tolerance.
- Define enterprise risk management.
- Define compliance risk management.

Before the Board begins this journey, the Board and the institution need to evaluate its level of risk tolerance and determine whether enterprise risk management or compliance risk management is the best assessment approach to evaluating institutional risk.

Primer on Risk

Risk surrounds us. Your institution is sued for a violation of Title IX (federal law prohibiting sex-based discrimination); your servers are hacked, and ransom is demanded; your President quits unexpectedly after a scandal. How your institution deals with these issues defines your level of risk tolerance.

There are four basic ways to deal with risk—avoid, mitigate, transfer, and assume. Keep in mind that assessing risk is on a continuum ranging from limited risk to high risk. The key is to understand this continuum and understand your role in assessing risk tolerance.

Avoid risk. Do not do anything that could create any risk to the institution. Disallow alcohol on campus; disapprove scuba diving courses; cancel study abroad programs; and approve all applications for promotion and tenure, even from unworthy candidates. Avoiding risk simply means to avoid anything that could possibly (even remotely) result in your institution being sued or creating any form of institutional or personal liability.

Mitigate risk. Identify the risk and put controls in place so that the potential negative effect of the risky activity is reduced. Allow alcohol at certain locations on campus and under certain conditions; offer widely popular scuba diving classes but require students to rent equipment from a professional, certified third-party provider; continue study abroad programs with evacuation procedures in place; and approve only applicants for promotion and tenure who have gone through a robust peer review and external screening process. To mitigate means to reduce the effect of the risk; it does not mean that an institution avoids all risk.

Transfer risk. Transferring the risk is all about determining how the institution is not the only entity, or the last one, left holding the bag when a lawsuit is filed. Make the provider of alcohol assume the liability for allowing underage drinking; make the provider of scuba equipment acknowledge its responsibility for faulty equipment; ensure that all students studying abroad have purchased their own health and evacuation insurance; and carry liability insurance to protect the institution when an angry faculty member who did not get tenure sues the institution alleging discrimination. Transferring risk is not just about purchasing insurance; it is also about putting other entities in front of the institution when the attorneys circle up, seeking to sue everyone and anyone for monetary damages.

Assume the risk. Your institution tried to avoid the risk, mitigate the risk, and transfer the risk. All risk that remains is what the institution assumes. So when a drunk student driver is injured in a car accident after a University-sanctioned party; the scuba equipment fails and a student drowns; a faculty member leading a study abroad program has a heart attack and medical evacuation is not available; and the lawsuit by the professor who was denied tenured is determined by the court system to be a valid claim - your institution could be held responsible for any uninsured costs.

Your institution is legally responsible for any fine/punishment resulting from a noncompliance issue where the "just say no" edict did not work (avoid the risk); where the risk could not be reduced by policy, practice, or working protocol (mitigate the risk); and where the risk could not be shifted to another entity agreeing to assume it (transfer the risk).

Ponder Moment

What risk philosophy best represents your institution? Does your institution avoid risk, proceed with caution after policies are in place, attempt to dump the risk on a third party, or realize that risk exists and assumes that risk? Or is your institution a combination of all the above?

Why does a Board need to understand its institutional risk tolerance? When a compliance initiative begins and the data surfaces, there will be disclosures of noncompliance and calls for remedying the various issues. Once the Board learns of noncompliance situations, the Board cannot simply ignore these situations; it must act. The Board will need to stand ready to make hard decisions as to which noncompliance issues can be avoided, mitigated, transferred, or assumed. Knowing your institution's level of risk tolerance before being faced with these issues will make those difficult decisions easier to put into long-term and short-term perspective.

Enterprise Risk Management or Compliance Risk Management

While contemplating your institution's level of risk tolerance, the question arises—what is the scope of this assessment? Is every possible risk and every possible horrible outcome assessed or is there a more measured identification of the risks and associated liability within the assessment? This is a decision for the President and Board.

Two different approaches are discussed below.

Enterprise Risk Management

With an enterprise risk management (ERM) approach, the institution assesses every risk that could impact the institution. This list ranges from a financial perspective to a reputational perspective to a compliance perspective; the list is endless and is customizable to each institution. Institutions that adopt an ERM mindset force themselves to take a broad-brush approach to look at all possible risks to not only the entity but also to its employees, its students, its Board, and possibly even to the larger society. Assessing these risks from a broad perspective then leads to the President or Board deciding on a path of action to mitigate the risks based on the institution's level of risk tolerance.

Compliance Risk Management

Compliance risk management is a single slice of ERM. Under this assessment model, the institution would identify the risk by identifying a specific law or regulation; assess the risk from the perspective of whether the institution is, or is not, in compliance with the law or regulation; and then develop a mitigation plan focusing on continuing to keep the institution in compliance with the identified law or regulation.

Obviously, compliance risk management has a much narrower focus than the ERM approach.

Differences and Similarities

ERM is broader in focus; compliance risk management is narrower in focus. Which focus is best for your institution? Before you jump into making that decision, the question must be asked—what exists presently at your institution? You don't want to, or need to, re-create what is presently in existence. And you don't want to start this initiative without gauging institutional commitment to developing and implementing a compliance initiative.

Bottom line, if your institution has no compliance risk assessment program, morphing into an ERM program and looking holistically at all possible risks and all possible resulting damage to the institution would be an exercise in futility. Your institution is simply not ready to take this giant leap to the moon. Consider instead focusing on identifying the federal, state, and local laws with which a higher education institution needs to comply and build your compliance risk assessment survey instruments to address those needs. Prioritize the risks that have the greatest potential impact on your institution in terms of potential reputational damage, property damage, or worse—possible injury or death of an employee or student. Once this system is in place for several assessment cycles, consider the possibility of broadening the method of your assessment to address a more holistic approach through an ERM process.

It is better to have a successful launch of a compliance risk assessment program with a narrow focus than to have a failed launch of a risk assessment program with a broad purpose. NASA had numerous space launch failures before finally sending Alan Shepard into space. Remember that the goal is long-term viability of a risk assessment compliance program.

Action Items:

1. Determine your institution's risk tolerance levels.
2. Decide if ERM or compliance risk management is the best approach.

CHAPTER 3

UNITED STATES SENTENCING GUIDELINES FOR ORGANIZATIONS—MAP FOR COMPLIANCE

CHAPTER GOALS:

- Understand the applicability of the United States Federal Sentencing Guidelines for Organizations to higher education institutions.
- Identify the seven elements of an effective compliance program.

A compliance risk initiative should be based on the Federal Sentencing Guidelines for Organizations,[3] which are the widely accepted best practices for developing an effective compliance program. Using these Guidelines to develop a customized compliance program for your institution will result in the initiative having immediate credibility.

Brief History

The Federal Sentencing Guidelines for Organizations is the product of the United States Sentencing Commission, which was created by the Sentencing Reform Act of 1984[4] (Title II of the Comprehensive Crime Control Act of 1984). Adopted in 1991, the Guidelines were designed to ensure that US-based "organizations" could not profit from wrongdoing and that organizations must implement appropriate compliance programs to prevent wrongdoing from occurring in the first place.

The Guidelines apply to any "organization," which is defined as "a person other than an individual," and those organizations include corporations, partnerships, associations, joint-stock companies, unions, trusts, pension funds, unincorporated organizations, governments and political subdivisions thereof, and nonprofit organizations. A higher education institution falls into this definition, whether private or public.

One of the Guidelines' primary goals was to alleviate sentencing disparities in the federal court system for individuals and organizations convicted of felonies and serious (Class A) misdemeanors. With a compliance program built into your institution's structure, a fine imposed against your institution for a criminal act could be reduced if the institution (1) has an effective compliance and ethics program and (2) has self-reported, cooperated, or accepted responsibility for its criminal activity.[5]

A Board discussion point should be the incorporation of an ethics component into your compliance initiative. The Guidelines use the term "compliance and ethics program." However, there is not clear guidance as to what the ethical component truly entails. An ethics component could include adopting an employee code of conduct; providing proactive training for how to handle an ethical dilemma; having an ethics hotline to report not only noncompliance with a law but also unacceptable behavior in the workplace; or other similar components focusing on the right thing to do rather than simply following the law. This is an institutional decision—just consider the different options before implementing the compliance initiative, including the option of starting with the focus on compliance and morphing into adding an ethics component within a few years.

Seven Elements Needed to Develop an Effective Compliance Program

The entire applicable statutory language of the Guidelines is in Appendix A. The abbreviated version of the seven elements of the Guidelines are below and include references to the chapters in this book where the specific element is discussed.

> *To have an effective compliance and ethics program, for purposes of subsection (f) of §8C2.5 (Culpability Score) and subsection (b)(1) of §8D1.4 (Recommended Conditions of Probation—Organizations), an organization shall—*
>
> *(1) exercise due diligence to prevent and detect criminal conduct; and*
>
> Chapter 6-Phase 3-Assessment Process
>
> *(2) otherwise promote an organizational culture that encourages ethical conduct and a commitment to compliance with the law.*
>
> Chapter 4—Phase 1—Compliance Structure
> Chapter 9—Integrating Other Guidelines
>
> *(3) use reasonable efforts not to include within the substantial authority personnel of the organization any individual whom the organization knew, or should have known, through the exercise of due diligence, engaged in illegal activities or other conduct inconsistent with an effective compliance and ethics program.*
>
> Chapter 9—Integrating Other Guidelines

(4) take reasonable steps to communicate periodically and in a practical manner its standards and procedures,

Chapter 9—Integrating Other Guidelines

(5) take reasonable steps (A) to ensure that the organization's compliance and ethics program is followed, . . . (B) to evaluate periodically the effectiveness of the organization's compliance and ethics program; and (C) to have and publicize a system, which may include mechanisms that allow for anonymity or confidentiality, whereby the organization's employees and agents may report or seek guidance regarding potential or actual criminal conduct without fear of retaliation.

Chapter 6—Phase 3—Assessment Process
Chapter 7—Phase 4—Mitigation Plan
Chapter 8—Phase 5—Monitor, Reassess, and Modify

(6) promote and enforce consistently a compliance and ethics program . . .

Chapter 9—Integrating Other Guideliness

(7) take reasonable steps to respond appropriately to the criminal conduct and to prevent further similar criminal conduct, including making any necessary modifications to the organization's compliance and ethics program. . . . periodically assess the risk of criminal conduct and shall take appropriate steps to design, implement, or modify each requirement . . . to reduce the risk of criminal conduct identified through this process.

Chapter 8—Phase 5—Monitor, Reassess, and Modify

The International Space Station began in 1998 with the launch of the Zarya control module. Since then, the massive structure in the sky has grown and grown. Your institution's compliance initiative starts with the Guidelines and can grow into a successful launch of a compliance program.

Action Items:

1. Discuss with the President if your institution is ready to launch a compliance program or a compliance and ethics program.
2. Confirm that your compliance (or compliance and ethics) program is based on the seven elements of the Guidelines.
3. Encourage publication of compliance program with references to the Guidelines. The references bring instant credibility since stakeholders know your institution is modeling this initiative after already-established best practices in the compliance field.

CHAPTER 4

PHASE ONE—COMPLIANCE STRUCTURE

CHAPTER GOALS:

- Understand the importance of compliance structure.
- Consider options for reporting lines to the Board.

There is no "one size fits all" compliance risk assessment initiative. The actual structure will depend upon a variety of variables—ranging from availability of personnel and resources to be committed, gauged interest and support of the Board and President, and the scope of the initial and continuing compliance efforts.

At a minimum, as specified in element 1 of the Guidelines, the structure must have high-level personnel who can garner the necessary campus wide buy-in and who will ensure that there is an effective compliance program. Specific individuals (think position, not person) must have assigned responsibility for the program.[6]

The Board is responsible for supporting and monitoring the compliance efforts. It is important that, whatever the structure your institution chooses, the head of that structure has unfettered access to the Board (or appropriately designated Board committee – perhaps the Audit Committee, Audit and Compliance Committee, or Compliance Committee). It is similarly important that the Board/Board committee adopt a charter/bylaws that clearly identify the responsibility of the Board/Board committee in this compliance effort and reporting lines. (See Appendix B for a sample Board Compliance Committee Charter). A governing Board has failed its fiduciary duty and its duty under the Guidelines when it fails to set up a system that allows for a direct (or dotted) reporting line from the highest-ranking compliance professional and/or compliance committee to the Board without any interference from anyone at the institution.

This reporting structure should result in an interactive process with regular communications flowing to and from the Board. The Board should receive regular updates on the identified compliance risks and what steps are being taken to mitigate the risks. If the Board does not know what the risks are, how can the Board adequately assist the institution in proactively addressing the risks and working toward a long-term sustainable compliance initiative? In addition, the Board should be involved in determining the institutional level of comfort with risk (see Chapter 2) and be aware of the financial implications of various assumed risks.

Tips:

- Ensure that the compliance initiative has clearly identified reporting lines on the institution's organizational chart. The level of importance of the compliance efforts will be assessed by the campus community based on this identified reporting structure.
- Consider if the institution's compliance professional should meet in-person with the Board, or appropriately designated Board committee, or if the information being provided by the

professional should be filtered through other layers. Consider if the Board, or committee, should meet with this professional if the individual is being terminated from the compliance position. The person in this position wields authority and is sometimes the bearer of bad news, and it is likely that not all recommendations will be warmly received. Ensure that there is a check-and-balance system for this compliance professional to have the responsibility and freedom to consistently pursue the right course of action even if such pursuit might mean stepping on toes.

Action Items:

1. Be knowledgeable of the compliance structure developed for your institution.
2. Develop and adopt a Board/Board Committee Charter that details the relationship of the Board/Board committee to the compliance initiative as well as the reporting requirements of the compliance initiative to the Board/Board committee.

CHAPTER 5

PHASE TWO—COMPLIANCE RISK UNIVERSE

CHAPTER GOALS:

- Understand what is a compliance risk universe.
- Identify resources to establish the scope of the compliance risk universe.

"Contrary to popular belief, NASA did not invent Teflon, Velcro or Tang. But it did invent flying to the moon."[7]

Just like NASA and the man-to-the-moon project, your institution is not inventing every element of your compliance initiative. So, what is the focus of your institution's compliance program?

An institution cannot design a compliance initiative until it decides what the scope of the project is. The Guidelines provide some direction by stating that an organization should promote a culture that encourages ethical conduct and a commitment to compliance with the law.[8] Within this broad mandate, your institution can customize its efforts to fit the needs. Will the scope be on only assessing compliance with federal laws or regulations or will the scope expand to include assessing compliance with institutional policies and procedures or even state and local laws?

How does the Board help with this decision on the scope of the project? Consider encouraging your institution to adopt best practices in higher education to identify what laws, rules, and regulations apply to your institution and how they should be assessed. There is no reason to reinvent the wheel; the work has already been done for your institution.

The simplest way for a higher education institution to define the scope is to find lists of federal, state, and local laws and regulations identified by other higher education institutions; discard those items not applicable to your institution; and assess all the remaining laws and regulations. Using predetermined lists of applicable laws from nationally recognized organizations provides instant credibility to your initiative. It is these lists that become the basis for a risk universe matrix.

Examples of preidentified lists that could form the basis for a compliance risk assessment are standards developed under OSHA, the EPA, or any other federal regulatory agency. The most comprehensive listing of federal laws that apply to an institution of higher education is the Higher Education Compliance Alliance (HECA) matrix, developed in conjunction with the National Association of College and University Attorneys (NACUA). Customizing this predetermined list will result in your institution being able to adopt this risk universe matrix that would represent best practices in the industry.

Another method to identify a risk universe matrix would be for your compliance professional/committee to conduct personal interviews with key institutional employees to determine what laws and regulations the institution must comply with on a daily, weekly, monthly, yearly, or multiyear basis. This method is, obviously, much more time-consuming than the option described above. However, it will provide an excellent opportunity for the compliance committee to hear the concerns faced by the employees who are charged with day-to-day operational compliance concerns.

A word of caution: If this latter method is the only means of identifying the risk universe matrix, it is possible that the managers being interviewed may not know what they do not know. In other words, they may be unintentionally ignorant. For example, does the employee being interviewed know all the laws relevant to that employee's area? What about laws that span across functional areas? These concerns can be dealt with by follow-up due diligence research—through additional conversations with the interviewees—as to what laws are applicable to a specific area in higher education.

What option your institution chooses will depend upon the size of the institution and the scope of the compliance effort. Customization is the continuing key word for all elements of this compliance risk assessment process. For example, your institution might start with assessing all federal laws in the area of human resources, or it might start with assessing all institutional policies and procedures in the area of financial affairs. Remember, initially starting with a manageable number of laws or regulations to assess will result in a more manageable compliance initiative that can be expanded upon in future years.

Another word of caution: The methodology for identifying the risk universe is not a Board decision. Rather this decision lies firmly in the hands of the compliance professional/committee charged with this responsibility. The role of the Board is to understand that a risk universe has been established; to encourage continuous reassessment of federal, state, and local laws and regulation to ensure that a robust list continues to be current; and to be supportive of this effort.

NASA was tasked with flying to the moon; the engineers had to know the scope of their project before they began. You are tasking your institution with developing a compliance initiative; the compliance committee must know the scope of its project before beginning development of a compliance risk universe.

Action Items:

1. Understand what risk universe matrix your institution is using.
2. Encourage use of established resources to develop the risk universe matrix.

CHAPTER 6

PHASE THREE—ASSESSMENT PROCESS

CHAPTER GOALS:

- Understand the assessment process.
- Understand the likelihood of occurrence and impact of occurrence factors.
- Comprehend the purpose of a heat map.
- Understand how to prioritize risk.

Navigating to and around the moon was a computing challenge—one that required the most advanced computers at MIT as well as human computers such as Katherine Johnson, the NASA mathematician celebrated in the book and movie "Hidden Figures."[9]

Just like NASA had a goal of reaching the moon, your institution has identified a goal—assessing the compliance risk universe. And just like NASA, your institution has identified the individuals who are responsible for navigating the risk assessment.

The actual assessment is not the role of the Board. The Board receives the information from the assessment and acts upon that information. However, the Board does need to understand and have faith in the assessment process. This chapter provides an overview of a compliance assessment process that, obviously, will be customized for your institution.

General Overview

After the institution determines its compliance structure (Chapter 4) and the scope of the compliance risk universe (Chapter 5), the institution moves into the next phase—assessing the risk of noncompliance. Assessment begins with surveying compliance with the identified risks.

Your institution will develop a survey instrument to assist in collecting compliance data. A typical survey instrument is divided into three main parts:

- Part 1 identifies present institutional polices, training, and procedures and also identifies how (or if) data collection is needed or if a physical inspection is required by law. Additionally, this section gathers information regarding the need for a disclosure or report sent to an outside agency.
- Part 2 focuses on identification of potential new or updated policies, training, and procedures that could be utilized to ensure compliance with the specific law. This section identifies best practices and changes in the law that require modifications in existing processes, policies, and training.
- Part 3 is an open-ended question used to identify any additional concerns and/or compliance risks that the institution

needs to be aware of to be fully compliant with a law. This section also serves to identify any barriers or obstacles that might prevent, or decrease, compliance with the law.

The individuals responsible for implementing the compliance program will review the answers to all the survey questions. They will look at whether there are policies or training in place, whether the fine for noncompliance is jail time or a slap on the wrist, whether the law needs to be complied with daily, or whether this law requires a simple report to an obscure agency every five years, etc. This evaluation will be done for each law that the institution identified to be assessed in the universe of risk.

The next step is to identify the level of compliance risk associated with each specific law. Two factors are analyzed to determine the level of risk to the institution - likelihood of occurrence and impact of occurrence.

Likelihood of occurrence is the probability that noncompliance with a law or regulation will occur daily, monthly, yearly, once every five years, once every ten years, etc. In other words, if incorrect data identified an employee as exempt and the employee should have been classified as nonexempt, every time that employee works overtime and does not get paid, this is a violation of a wage and hour law—a compliance violation.

Figure 1: Sample—Likelihood of Occurrence Factors

Likelihood of Occurrence Factors			
Rank/Scale		Measure of Likelihood	
		Existing Controls	Frequency of Non-Compliance
1	Rare	• Policies mandated and updated regularly. • Regular mandatory training is provided to the identified responsible person(s) and is documented. • Regular management monitoring reviews are performed and documented.	May only occur in exceptional circumstances Less than once in 10 years
2	Unlikely	• Policies mandated and updated regularly. • Regular training is provided to the identified responsible person(s), but not documented. • Regular management monitoring reviews are performed, but not documented.	Could occur at some time At least once in 10 years
3	Possible	• Policies mandated, but not updated regularly. • Responsible person(s) identified. • Training is provided when needed. • Some management monitoring reviews are performed, but not documented.	Might occur at some time At least once in 5 years
4	Likely	• Policies and procedures in place but neither mandated nor updated regularly. • Responsible person(s) identified. • Some formal and informal (on the job) training. • No management monitoring reviews.	Will probably occur At least once per year
5	Almost Certain	• No controls in place. • No policies or procedures, no responsible person(s) identified, no training, and no management monitoring reviews.	Expected to occur in most circumstances More than once per year

Impact of occurrence is the probability that a noncompliant incident will have a certain effect on the institution in terms of financial resources being depleted, the institution being fined by a regulatory agency, damage to the institution's reputation occurring in the eyes of the public, or even a more practical example—a loss of utilization of a building due to a mercury spill on the main floor.

The compliance committee will review the survey data and will determine the likelihood of occurrence and the impact of occurrence for each identified and assessed law. Since this committee understands its role of identifying to the institution the risks associated with noncompliance, the data produced by this risk analysis must be assessed, ranked in order of risk level using the likelihood of occurrence and impact of occurrence factors, and then displayed in a manner in which the President can understand what risks are facing the institution. It is then the decision of the President as to how to present this information to the Board.

To accomplish compiling the information into a usable format, the compliance committee assigns a number to the factor of likelihood of occurrence and a number to the factor of impact of occurrence. Each institution determines the numerical scale for these factors. For example, with the factor of likelihood of occurrence, the institution may decide to use a one-to-five scale to assess this factor. Using this scale, the compliance committee might assign a "one" to a particular law. This "one" would refer to the fact that there is a likelihood that noncompliance will occur once every ten years while a "five" would refer to the fact that there is a likelihood that noncompliance will occur daily. Similarly, with the factor of impact of occurrence, the compliance committee might assign a "three" to a particular law, using a one-to-ten scale. In this example, a "three" means the impact on the institution of noncompliance would be fairly minimal in contrast to an assigned "ten," which would mean that the impact would be catastrophic, including closing the institution. (See Figure 1 for the likelihood-of-occurrence template and Figure 2 for the impact-of-occurrence template.)

Figure 2: Sample—Impact of Occurrence Factors

Impact of Occurrence Factors								
Rank/Scale		Measure of Impact						
		Legal/ Compliance	Health and Safety	Financial		Strategic	Potential Disruption of Business Operations	Reputation and Image
				Monetary	Assets			
1	Insignificant	In compliance	No injuries	TBD dollar amount or percentage of budget	Little or no impact	Little or no impact	< ½ day	Unsubstantiated, low impact, low profile or no news items
2	Minor	Civil violation with little/no fines	First aid treatment	TBD dollar amount or percentage of budget	Minor loss or damage	Minor impact	< 1 day	Substantiated, low impact, low news profile
3	Serious	Significant civil fines/penalties	Medical treatment	TBD dollar amount or percentage of budget	Major damage	Major impact	1 day-1 week	Substantiated, public embarrassment, moderate impact, moderate news profile
4	Disastrous	Serious violation, criminal prosecution probable	Death or extensive injuries	TBD dollar amount or percentage of budget	Significant loss	Significant impact	1 week-1 month	Substantiated, public embarrassment, high impact, high news profile, third party actions
5	Catastrophic	Significant violation, criminal conviction probable, loss of accreditation or licensure	Multiple deaths or several permanent disabilities	TBD dollar amount or percentage of budget	Complete loss of assets	Loss of accreditati on or license	> 1 month	Substantiated, public embarrassment, very high multiple impacts, high widespread news profile, third party actions

Obviously, customization of the scale is required. However, regardless of how the institution customizes the scale, ultimately, the assigned number ratings must be added up and displayed on a document that is typically called a heatmap.

The heatmap is a simple addition of the numerical ratings of all the occurrence factors and likelihood factors for each law. The math is simple—add up the "points" (scale) assigned to each risk factor and come up with a total score. Then plot those scores on a heatmap. (See Figure 3 for a heatmap template, with a dot indicating the location of assessments detailed below).

Figure 3: Sample—Heat Map

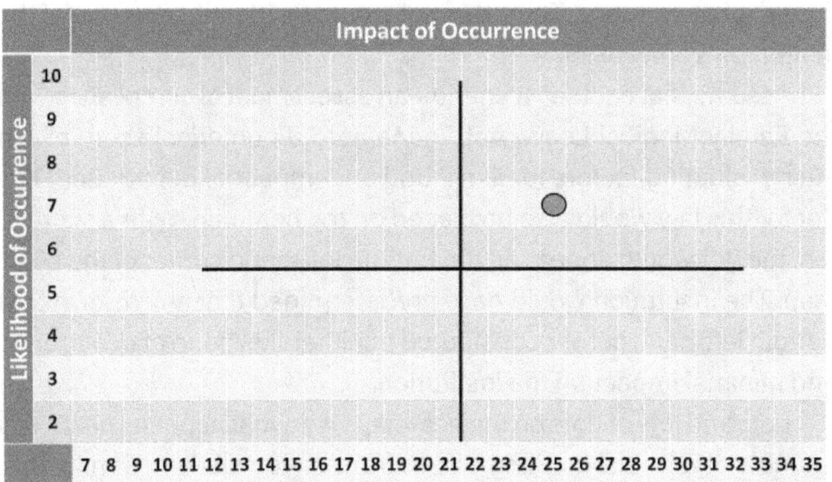

Imagine this scenario: The institution is evaluating its compliance with Title IX, the law that prohibits sexual harassment. The institution has already agreed on the likelihood and impact using numerical scales. Using a likelihood of impact scale and an impact of occurrence scale and assigning a numerical value under each of those scales, the numbers add up to a combined thirty-five. That combined score of thirty-five would appear as a dot on the heatmap. And since that number is a thirty-five, this dot would land in the top right-hand corner of the heatmap.

Think of the heat map as divided into four quadrants. The top right-hand corner is for risks that have a high likelihood of occurring, with high impact on the institution. The bottom left-hand corner is for risks that have minimal likelihood of occurring and, if the risk did result in an occurrence, the occurrence would have minimal impact on the institution in terms of financial, legal, reputational, or operational results (or whatever other factors your institution determines relevant for assessing impact).

The institution would have predetermined the importance of each quadrant. In this scenario, the institution has determined that any dot that lands in the top right-hand quadrant of the heatmap is in an area designated as having a high likelihood of occurrence and a high impact of occurrence. Thus, this dot would be identified as one of the institution's chief risks.

Assume that another scenario—an assessment of compliance with the Family Medical Leave Act—generated a numerical score of ten after evaluating factors for likelihood and impact of occurrence. The dot for this law would also be placed on the heatmap. With a score of ten, the dot would appear on the bottom left-hand corner of the heatmap. The institution would have predetermined that any risks in that bottom left-hand corner constituted minimal likelihood of occurrence and minimal impact on the institution.

Lots and lots of dots on the heatmap—so, what happens next? You are now at a Board meeting and in front of you sits a heatmap with lots of dots that reference specific laws that were assessed by the compliance committee. The heatmap looks complicated. Knowing that an institution has limited time and resources, the question becomes this: Which risk does the institution attack?

The plan to mitigate and prioritize the risks is discussed in Chapter 7.

Action Items:

1. Approve the assessment process, including likelihood of occurrence and impact of occurrence factors.
2. Endorse the concept of utilization of the heatmap.

CHAPTER 7

PHASE FOUR—MITIGATION PLAN

CHAPTER GOALS:

- Understand how to interpret a heatmap of risk levels.
- Understand how to prioritize risks.

"OK, Houston, we've had a problem here." Those were words spoken during a communication between Apollo 13 astronaut Jack Swigert and NASA's Mission Control Center in Houston that signified that an explosion had crippled their spacecraft. Houston's response focused on how to mitigate the situation, safely land the spacecraft, and save the lives of its astronauts.

"Houston, we have a problem" is the popular phrase frequently used to identify the emergence of an unforeseen problem underscored with a sense of urgency depending on what the problem is. Now, similar to what NASA Mission Control had to do, the institution has identified the issue(s) using the compliance risk assessment survey, has identified the likelihood and impact on the institution by using the compliance risk factors, and now must work to develop a mitigation plan to address the risk.

Each law that is assessed requires its own mitigation plan. A mitigation plan identifies the noncompliance factors associated with a specific law and then designs a detailed plan to address the issue and mitigate the risk to the institution. The length and complexity of the plan varies. At minimum, the plan would identify the noncompliance issues and what would be needed to reduce the risk. For example, there might be a need for training institutional employees, for new software, for a new position, or other remedial actions. In addition, the plan would detail costs associated with the "fix" and the estimated time to start and complete the mitigation aspects.

After the heatmap is done and all the mitigation plans are developed, it is at this phase of the compliance initiative when the decisions regarding the acceptable level of risk tolerance by the Board and the institution are relevant. Obviously, all laws need to always be complied with; however, is that compliance level achievable and feasible?

So, how does an institution prioritize the risks? Various approaches can be used.

High-Risk-Only Focus

This approach focuses *solely* on the dot or dots in the upper right-hand quadrant of the heatmap. With this focus comes the presumption that any risk identifications making it to this area are of such a catastrophic compliance risk to the institution that the risk must be mitigated above all others, whatever the cost, time, or effort. Other risks are acknowledged but remain a low priority to address.

Under this approach, there might be a tendency to be lulled into complacency by the idea that once these risks are mitigated, there will be no other risks and the institution can stop the compliance initiative. Obviously, this is not correct. All risks are never totally eliminated, and new risks arise all the time. And by not at least monitoring mid- or low-level risks, possible noncompliance issues could arise without warning, or existing risks could worsen without proper attention.

All-Risk Focus

If your institution exists in a perfect utopia with unlimited time and resources, this approach is realistic. The approach is premised on the fact that the institution would address *all* the identified compliance risks and mitigate them all at the same time.

Obviously, your institution should always comply with all federal, state, and local laws. But, quite honestly, not all compliance risks are equal. In the Apollo 13 launch, Commander Mattingly was replaced right before the launch due to exposure to the rubella virus. Three days after lift-off, an explosion occurred on the spacecraft, resulting in an emergency engineering redesign to filter air.[10] Commander Mattingly never developed rubella. Both are risks, but clearly the possibility of running out of air equates to the higher risk.

It is the same for institutions. For example, institutions are required to comply with Constitution Day, which is the federally designated one-day event to recognize the adoption of the US Constitution and those who have become US citizens.[11] Noncompliance with this law would result in a watchdog organization highlighting the institution on social media and possible (but extremely unlikely and has not occurred in the history of this law) loss of the institution's ability to award federal financial aid. Compliance with this law is easy to attain. Simply put a patriotic display of books at the library or have an employee read the Constitution on your campus grounds.

In contrast, compliance with Title IX is much more difficult. This law requires an institution to protect its employees and students against sexual harassment and discrimination based on sex. Title IX situations could occur daily, weekly, or monthly. Policies to ensure compliance with Title IX contain numerous pages detailing complicated due process procedures that an institution must follow to protect both the complainant and respondent. The likelihood of occurrence of noncompliance is high due to the uncertainty of when and how many Title IX allegations will arise. There could be significant impact on the institution in terms of noncompliance resulting in disgruntled employees and students, complaints filed with the Office of Civil Rights, lawsuits, and negative publicity.

As is evident, the impact of noncompliance would be significantly higher in dealing with Title IX compared with the impact of noncompliance with the requirements of Constitution Day. But with the all-risk approach, all risks must be mitigated and resolved.

The impact on your institution with this approach may be a poor use of time and resources. This approach is achievable for an institution with unlimited resources and unlimited personnel with time to spend on mitigating all compliance risks. If your institution does not have this level of resources, perhaps an all-risk focus may not be the best option.

High-Risk Focus, Awareness of Midlevel Dangers, Acknowledgment of Low-Level Risk

This approach combines the prioritization of the highest risks, with a moderate and measured response to the midlevel risk, and acknowledgment of the low-level risk. In this approach, the prioritization focuses on high-risk compliance issues coupled with empowerment given to the compliance committee to identify how midlevel risks could be mitigated, eliminated, or managed with limited expenditure of time and resources. Low-level risks are not ignored; they are simply not prioritized for day-to-day work. Rather, these compliance risks are ones the institutional personnel will work toward mitigating sometime in the future.

Consider these scenarios. First scenario—the institution has completed an assessment of all federal laws that deal with student affairs. The assessment reveals that the institution's Americans with

Disabilities Act policy is significantly out of compliance with the federal regulations. At minimum, the work to be accomplished to achieve compliance will involve rewriting the policy, training all ADA staff, rebuilding faith in the process with faculty, and designing proactive training programs for campus constituents. All these noncompliant issues create a very high risk of likelihood of occurrence of lawsuits against the institution with a high financial and reputational impact on the institution. This noncompliance "dot" will appear in the top right-hand quadrant of the heat map. This noncompliance could result in the hiring of a full-time ADA coordinator even at the cost of other projects not being funded.

Second scenario—the institution has completed an assessment of all federal laws that deal with human resources issues. As a result of the assessment, the institution realizes that employees are receiving fewer Family Medical Leave Act benefit weeks than are required by law. Noncompliance due to lack of process is identified; midlevel risk to the institution in terms of possible fines and likelihood of occurrence is identified; and a mitigation plan is developed and implemented, resulting in the purchase of a relatively low-cost calendaring system.

In this type of approach, priority for implementation of mitigation plans will focus on the high-risk compliance issues with awareness of the midlevel risk. This would be a compromise system that might work within the institution's limited monetary and staffing resources.

Caution

A word of caution—depending on the scope of the universe of risk to be assessed, it is possible that the initial institution's compliance risk assessment could result in a very high number of identified compliance risks and resulting mitigation plans. This is not the moment to be discouraged. Rather, this is the moment to acknowledge that the institution is tackling a big problem that can be solved.

During the Apollo 13 flight, because of faulty electrical wiring, the crew lost valuable oxygen. Mission Control used only items that would be on the spaceship to devise a workable solution to the problem. Just like Apollo 13, the institution has limited resources. The Board needs to encourage and support the compliance initiative members to use those limited resources and work toward a solution in developing usable mitigation plans.

Regardless of which risk analysis an institution chooses, the Board and upper administration will face a moment or two of grave concern. This moment will occur when the institution determines its universe of risk, completes the assessment of the various laws, identifies the risk factors, assigns numerical values to the likelihood of occurrence and the impact of occurrence, and places the dots on the heatmap. It is very possible that this heatmap, and attached risk-mitigation plans, will have numerous dots, including dots in the top right-hand quadrant.

While this could cause management and the Board to be very nervous, the better way to look at the data is to acknowledge that noncompliance has occurred, but the institution has a plan to fix it. Having a robust compliance program that identifies these known risks is better than ignoring the issues and just hoping for the best. Mission Control could not ignore the loss of the oxygen, and neither could the crew. The Board also cannot ignore the institution's risks.

Action Items:

1. Be involved in the discussion regarding how the institution prioritizes risk.
2. Discuss and determine the level of Board review of mitigation plans.

CHAPTER 8

PHASE FIVE—MONITOR, REASSESS, AND MODIFY

CHAPTER GOALS:

- Understand why continual compliance risk monitoring is needed.
- Understand the need to develop a customized system to continuously monitor the compliance risk assessment initiative.
- Explore the timing of the compliance risk reassessment schedule.

Vast stretches of the unknown and the unanswered and the unfinished still far outstrip our collective comprehension.[12]

—John F. Kennedy

The institution has developed the compliance structure (Chapter 4); has identified the universe of risk (Chapter 5); has implemented the survey assessment and identified a numerical scale to assess the likelihood of occurrence and impact of occurrence on the institution (Chapter 6); has compiled mitigation plans and has determined how to prioritize the identified risks (Chapter 7), and now must look toward the future in developing a method of continuous monitoring and assessment, with modifications as needed.

So what is next for the institution? President Kennedy's quote above reminds the reader that humans need to look toward the future and explore the "vast stretches of the unknown." The work of the compliance initiative has just begun.

The Guidelines clearly identify the element of "internal compliance monitoring" as a requirement for an effective compliance program.[13] Laws change; employees change; Boards change. The fact that change will occur is predicted; the unknown is how the Board and the institution will adapt to the changes and how to continue to ensure continued compliance with the laws. Just like the heat shield protecting the astronauts, the mechanism for internal compliance monitoring must be built to withstand a certain degree of pressure while also being nimble for changing conditions.

The key is having a continuous improvement system in place that provides enough flexibility to adapt to a changing environment. But the key is also having enough rigidity in the system to ensure that the compliance initiative will not falter when the new President arrives and wants to go in a different direction.

Monitor

The first step is developing a continuous compliance risk monitoring process. As a Board member, consider asking the following questions to fellow Board members and to members of the upper administration:

- Has the institution developed a calendar with required compliance reporting dates?
- Has this important function of compliance been written into applicable employee job descriptions?
- How often should reports from the compliance committee be presented to the Board?
- Have the employees responsible for monitoring compliance with a particular law been given the resources and training to ensure that their knowledge of the law can equate to institutional compliance with the law?
- Does the institution have a Reporting Policy (Whistleblower Policy)?
- Does the institution have and publicize a system for reporting noncompliance? A method for anonymous reporting must also be included.[14]
- Does the institution have an overarching Nonretaliation Policy? Does it include a prohibition against retaliation for reporting under the Reporting Policy?

Ask probing questions regarding the status of the mitigation plans.

Here are some things to ponder: What level of detail does the Board want/need in terms of reviewing and/or approving the mitigation plans? Does the Board simply want to see the dots on the heatmap and know that there are identified risks? Does the Board want to see the mitigation plan for all the identified risks or just certain risks? At some point, the Board's review of mitigation plans is certainly going into the weeds. This would result in the Board operating at a management level which is not the level at which a Board should act. So, at some point during this compliance initiative, discussion must occur between the Board and President regarding what level of Board review is appropriate.

It is not the role of the Board to manage mitigation plans; however, it is the fiduciary role of the Board to ensure their timely completion.

Reassess

The second step focuses on the implementation of a reassessment cycle. As a Board member, consider asking the following questions to fellow Board members and to upper administration members:

- How often is the institution completing a risk assessment?
- How often will the Board hear reports about the status of ongoing compliance risk assessment?
- How often should the Board meet to discuss risk tolerance?

Modify

The final step focuses on modification of the compliance risk initiative. As a Board member, consider asking the following questions to fellow Board members and to upper administration members:

- What changes have been made to the level of risk associated with a particular law based on the mitigation plan?
- What resources are needed to support modifications of the compliance program?
- Have employee discipline trends been analyzed? This question is important to ask because the trends tell a story of what policies and trainings are not in place to proactively avoid employee disciplinary actions. Which law or laws are being violated on a regular basis? Are institutional hiring practices causing the problem, or is it a lack of a reporting policy, or is it a lack of clearly written Guidelines for acceptable behavior? Determining the *why* will help to modify existing practices.

Management needs to *monitor* the compliance initiative. The Board needs to publicly support the initiative and ask relevant questions to ascertain the status of the initiative. Management needs to *reassess* policies, procedures, and training when a law changes or when new laws are enacted. The Board needs to understand why reassessment is occurring. Board members need to have appropriate training to ensure understanding of their roles in the compliance effort. Upper administration members need to *modify* the scope of the compliance risk initiative and mitigation plans as needed to continue to have an effective (and hopefully proactive) compliance program. The Board needs to continue to provide oversight of the compliance initiative to ensure the successful continuation of the program.

"Surely the opening vistas of space promise high costs and hardships, as well as high reward," said John F. Kennedy. [15] Conducting a risk assessment promises a high reward of ensuring the institution's compliance with the law and the Board's fulfillment of its fiduciary responsibilities. It also promises that the institution and the Board will spend considerable time and effort fostering a culture of compliance. Focus on getting to the moon.

Action Items:

1. Seek regular updates of compliance risks and actions taken as part of mitigation plans.
2. Be supportive of the need to reassess and modify the existing compliance initiative.
3. Encourage the continuation of a sustainable compliance initiative, which should be integrated into the culture of the institution.

CHAPTER 9

INTEGRATION OF OTHER FEDERAL SENTENCING GUIDELINE ELEMENTS

CHAPTER GOALS:

- Understand all the Guidelines.
- Know the Board's role in implementing a compliance initiative.

According to the Guidelines, the institution will "exercise due diligence to prevent and detect criminal conduct."[16] Remember that the Guidelines are the gold standard for best practices in establishing a robust and effective compliance program. To better reflect their mission, institutions should substitute wording that better reflects the institution's mission - "exercise due diligence to prevent and detect noncompliance with federal, state, and local laws as well as institutional policies."

Chapters 4 through 8 focused on the development and implementation of a compliance risk assessment, development of a mitigation plan resulting from the assessment, and the continuous process of monitoring, reassessing, and modifying the compliance program. This chapter explains the other elements in the Guidelines that support a compliance initiative.

Hiring Practices

The Guidelines require that the institution use reasonable efforts not to hire "substantial authority personnel" whom the organization knew, or should have known, engaged in illegal activities or other conduct inconsistent with an effective compliance and ethics program.[17] In other words, the institution should have clear processes to vet prospective employees and to hire individuals who embrace the overall concept of compliance. Indeed, even Board members should be vetted with this philosophy in mind rather than simply evaluated according to what prestige or financial support a potential Board member's presence brings to the table.

And if your institution does hire employees lacking a compliance mindset, would anyone be surprised if noncompliance issues arose? Hiring and retaining ethical employees who follow the law not simply because it is the legal course of action but rather because it is the right thing to do should be the institution's goal.

So, Board members, you should ask the question: What are the hiring practices? The institution needs to do a good job vetting the applicants, and ultimately employees, who will be able to head your effective compliance and ethics program.

Written Standards and Procedures

According to the Guidelines, for an organization to have an effective compliance program, the organization must have written standards and procedures and must communicate those standards and procedures to its employees.[18]

This requirement sounds easy, right? Just write standards down, have employees sign the Employee Handbook on the first day of employment, and incorporate the standards into regular employee training. Of course, all these steps will be done, and the compliance program will be successful.

Just in case it is possible that this scenario does not proceed so smoothly, it is important to remember that clearly articulated policies are the backbone of a compliance initiative. The Guidelines express an expectation that an employer develop acceptable standards of behavior and communicate those standards to the employees. The Guidelines say the employer should provide resources to ensure that employees know how to comply with the law and should communicate the availability of those resources to the employees. And note that a lack of resources (budget, time, and personnel) are not excusable reasons for an institution not to provide training to any employee.

How do Board members show their support for this important element? Perhaps by not rolling their eyes or laughing when the administration rolls out a policy on policies—that would be a good start. Board members should understand the critical nature of providing transparency and consistency when developing an institutional procedure on policies. They should ask questions as to why some policies should be Board-approved (overarching Nondiscrimination Policy) and why some should be approved at the Presidential or division level (Missing Student Policy). Board members should question where policies are housed (Employee Handbook or internal portal) to ensure that employees really can access the information. They should seek answers to what other institutions are doing in their compliance initiatives in terms of training and communication of written standards.

Training and Education

The Guidelines specify that an organization must conduct effective training programs.[19] No one reading this book should be surprised that the Guidelines emphasize training and education. Any initiative will fail without the institution providing appropriate training to employees who need to understand a specific topic/policy/process.

But don't forget that Board members need training as well. Do all Board members know what a compliance initiative is, what a Board member is required to disclose to avoid a conflict-of-interest dilemma, and even what the institution's procedure for communicating with news reporters is? Boards are integral to the success of the institution. Board members need to understand their role which can be achieved through robust and regularly scheduled educational sessions.

Compliance Program Communication

The Guidelines state that to have an effective compliance program, the organization must take reasonable measures to communicate periodically and in a reasonable manner about the elements of the compliance program.[20]

Failing to explain "why" the institution needs a compliance initiative; "who" is supporting the initiative; "where" information about the program is housed; and "when" various elements will be implemented could cause employees to become unreasonably negative toward the design, rollout, and implementation of a compliance program. Board members should not only discuss the compliance initiative regularly in their meetings but also should publicly and with transparency share their support of the compliance initiative as often as possible. They should encourage the President to keep employees regularly informed about what is happening with a compliance program to reduce resistance to the initiative.

Publicized Standards and Discipline

The Guidelines require that an effective compliance program "have and publicize a system, which may include mechanisms that allow for anonymity or confidentiality, whereby the organization's employees and agents may report or seek guidance regarding potential or actual criminal conduct without fear of retaliation."[21] This is truly a simple mandate and one that must have Board support and involvement.

The Board needs to encourage the President to ensure these policies are in place, and Board members need to remind themselves of their own responsibility to comply with all applicable institutional policies. For example, if you were asked to explain FERPA[22] or Title IX and the need for your compliance with these laws, what would be your response? Do you know what would constitute a conflict of interest between yourself and the institution? Would you know how to report a possible noncompliance issue? Presuming that the answer to at least one of these questions is a resounding "not sure," perhaps securing education and training on these and other subjects should be a Board goal.

Action Items:

1. Ask questions to ensure an understanding of the compliance initiative.
2. Support the development of a transparent policy process.
3. Be involved in the communication process to show continued support for the compliance initiative.
4. Actively encourage training and education of employees and Board members.

Published Standards and Disciplines

CHAPTER 10

CONCLUSION

> Many years ago, the great British explorer George Mallory, who was to die on Mount Everest, was asked why did he want to climb it. He said, "Because it is there."
>
> Well, space is there, and we're going to climb it, and the moon and the planets are there, and new hopes for knowledge and peace are there. And, therefore, as we set sail we ask God's blessing on the most hazardous and dangerous and greatest adventure on which man has ever embarked.[23]
>
> –John F. Kennedy

While it's almost certain that a compliance initiative is not the most hazardous and dangerous and greatest adventure upon which your institution has embarked, it's likely to be an adventure, nonetheless.

Be prepared for resistance from some faculty and staff members as well as administrators who don't want to change the status quo because "we always do it this way." Be aware that the assessment process will uncover flaws in systems, policies, and processes that the institution's executives may not want disclosed. Understand that these flaws, left unresolved, could result in fines against the institution. Commit to supporting funding for the initiatives for training, needed software, and other relevant needs identified in mitigation plans. Plan Board meetings with sufficient time to hear updates, to talk about risk tolerance, and to keep abreast of changes in laws that would affect your institution.

As stated throughout this book, customization of this process is the best course of action. What works at your institution? A full rollout of an assessment of all applicable federal laws; a partial assessment of laws applicable to one department; a push from the President with clear and visible Board support; a grassroots initiative that stirs up support? There is no wrong answer except the answer to not start.

> "The backers of Apollo may have made a fundamental strategic error: They framed the enterprise as a race. They won it—and then didn't know what to do next," wrote Joel Achenbach in a June 19, 2019, newspaper article.[24]

A compliance initiative is not a race. It is a never-ending marathon with cycles and loops. It is a systematic process based on the Federal Sentencing Guidelines and best practices, and it is designed to develop an effective ethics and compliance program that will strengthen institutional compliance with federal, state, and local laws and institutional policies.

NASA didn't put a man on the moon in a year. It took years, with multiple failures and successes, to reach the final goal. Boards need to embrace this long-term mentality that the initiative will have failures and successes. Ultimately, the institution, with support from the Board, will put the man on the moon by developing a robust and effective compliance program.

Good luck on your moon landing!

APPENDIX A

UNITED STATES FEDERAL SENTENCING GUIDELINES FOR ORGANIZATIONS

(USSG Sec. 2D1.1)

To have an effective compliance and ethics program, for purposes of subsection (f) of §8C2.5 (Culpability Score) and subsection (b)(1) of §8D1.4 (Recommended Conditions of Probation—Organizations), an organization shall—

(1) exercise due diligence to prevent and detect criminal conduct; and

(2) otherwise promote an organizational culture that encourages ethical conduct and a commitment to compliance with the law. Such compliance and ethics programs shall be reasonably designed, implemented, and enforced so that the program is generally effective in preventing and detecting criminal conduct. The failure to prevent or detect the instant offense

does not necessarily mean that the program is not generally effective in preventing and detecting criminal conduct. Due diligence and the promotion of an organizational culture that encourages ethical conduct and a commitment to compliance with the law within the meaning of subsection (a) minimally require the following:

> (1) The organization shall establish standards and procedures to prevent and detect criminal conduct.[25]
>
> (2) (A) The organization's governing authority shall be knowledgeable about the content and operation of the compliance and ethics program and shall exercise reasonable oversight with respect to the implementation and effectiveness of the compliance and ethics program.
>
> (B) High-level personnel of the organization shall ensure that the organization has an effective compliance and ethics program, as described in this guideline. Specific individual(s) within high-level personnel shall be assigned over-all responsibility for the compliance and ethics program.
>
> (C) Specific individual(s) within the organization shall be delegated day-to-day operational responsibility for the compliance and ethics program. Individual(s) with operational responsibility shall report periodically to high-level personnel and, as appropriate, to the governing authority, or an appropriate subgroup of the governing authority, on the effectiveness of the compliance and ethics program. To carry out such operational responsibility, such individual(s) shall be given adequate resources, appropriate authority, and direct access to the governing authority or an appropriate subgroup of the governing authority.[26]

(3) The organization shall use reasonable efforts not to include within the substantial authority personnel of the organization any individual whom the organization knew, or should have known through the exercise of due diligence, engaged in illegal activities or other conduct inconsistent with an effective compliance and ethics program.[27]

(4) (A) The organization shall take reasonable steps to communicate periodically and in a practical manner its standards and procedures, and other aspects of the compliance and ethics program, to the individuals referred to in subparagraph (B) by conducting effective training programs and otherwise disseminating information appropriate to such individuals' respective roles and responsibilities. The individuals referred to in subparagraph (A) are the members of the governing authority, high-level personnel, substantial authority personnel, the organization's employees, and, as appropriate, the organization's agents.[28]

(5) The organization shall take reasonable steps—

(A) to ensure that the organization's compliance and ethics program is followed, including monitoring and auditing to detect criminal conduct;[29]

(B) to evaluate periodically the effectiveness of the organization's compliance and ethics program; and[30]

(C) to have and publicize a system, which may include mechanisms that allow for anonymity or confidentiality, whereby the organization's employees and agents may report or seek guidance regarding potential or actual criminal conduct without fear of retaliation.[31]

(6) The organization's compliance and ethics program shall be promoted and enforced consistently throughout the organization through (A) appropriate incentives to perform in accordance with the compliance and ethics program; and (B) appropriate disciplinary measures for engaging in criminal conduct and for failing to take reasonable steps to prevent or detect criminal conduct.[32]

(7) After criminal conduct has been detected, the organization shall take reasonable steps to respond appropriately to the criminal conduct and to prevent further similar criminal conduct, including making any necessary modifications to the organization's compliance and ethics program. In implementing subsection (b), the organization shall periodically assess the risk of criminal conduct and shall take appropriate steps to design, implement, or modify each requirement set forth in sub-section (b) to reduce the risk of criminal conduct identified through this process.[33]

APPENDIX B

SAMPLE—BOARD COMPLIANCE COMMITTEE CHARTER

Note: This is a sample document designed to assist in the writing of your Board Compliance Committee Charter. Due to space limitations, certain sections that would normally appear in a charter have been eliminated—for example, membership, functions of the committee chair, committee meetings, and establishment of subcommittees.

1. Purpose:

The Compliance Committee (the "Committee") of the Board of XXX (the "College") will represent and assist the Board with the oversight of (a) the College's compliance with legal and regulatory requirements and (b) implementation of the College's Conflicts of Interest Policy.

2. Responsibilities and Processes:

The following will be the primary responsibilities of the Committee as it pertains to compliance.

(a) Ensure that the proper tone for compliance and ethics is established.

(b) Provide oversight as needed to ensure that the compliance and ethics program effectively prevents and detects instances of noncompliance by employees and officers of the College and encourages reporting of such instances.

(c) Monitor compliance with the College's Conflicts of Interest Policy.

(d) In cooperation with the College's Chief Ethics and Compliance Officer, monitor compliance with the reporting policy and receive reports, as appropriate and necessary, of alleged noncompliance with laws, regulations, and College policies by the Board, faculty, staff, students, and anyone doing business for or with the College.

(e) Assess the effectiveness of management's system for receiving and resolving allegations pertaining to noncompliance with law, policy, and procedures and assess the effectiveness of reporting mechanisms.

(f) Meet with the President on a periodic basis to review compliance risk assessments, action plans, and other steps to ensure the management of an effective compliance function.

(g) Meet with the Chief Ethics and Compliance Officer on a periodic basis to review the effectiveness of the compliance function.

APPENDIX C

SAMPLE—RISK ASSESSMENT SURVEY

STEP I
Identify Present Controls

This step is designed to identify *present* policies, education/training, and procedures that are in place now to ensure compliance with the above-stated law. Please answer as clearly and concisely as possible; the goal is to provide full and open disclosure of our present practices. This step is not to place blame; this step is designed to identify present controls.

Written Policy

- Does XX have a *written policy* in place to ensure compliance with the above-stated law? ☐ Y ☐ N ☐ N/A
- If yes:
    - Name of policy
    - Policy description

Training

- Does XX have *training* to ensure compliance with the above-stated law? ☐Y ☐N ☐N/A
- If yes:
  - Describe training
  - Who is trained?
  - Is the training mandatory? ☐Y ☐N
  - How is completion of training documented?
  - How is the training conducted?
  - ☐Informal (on-the-job training) ☐formal or ☐both
  - How often is training conducted?
  - Is there any independent verification of training? ☐Y ☐N
    - If yes:
    - Identify how training is independently verified
    - Provide education/training information not provided above

Compliance Procedures

- Does XX have *procedures* to ensure compliance with the above-stated law? ☐Y ☐N ☐N/A
- If yes:
  - Name of procedures
  - Procedures description

Disclosure

- Is disclosure/filing a report (either internal or external) required? ☐Y ☐N ☐N/A
- If yes:
  - Describe disclosure/report to be filed.
  - How often must reports be filed? (once, yearly, etc.)
  - Who files the report?

- Is there an independent review before it is filed? ☐ Y ☐ N
    - If yes:
        - Identify who independently reviews
        - Identify how the report is independently reviewed
- Provide disclosure/filing information not provided above

Data Collection

- Is data collection required by law? ☐ Y ☐ N ☐ N/A
- If yes:
    - Describe data collected
    - List person who collects data
    - How often is the data collected? (once, yearly, etc.)
    - Is there any independent review of the data? ☐ Y ☐ N
        - If yes:
            - Identify who independently reviews
            - Identify how data is independently reviewed
    - Provide data collection information not provided above

Physical Inspection

- Is a physical inspection required by law? ☐ Y ☐ N ☐ N/A
- If yes:
    - Describe inspection
    - Who does the inspection?
    - How often do inspections take place? (once, yearly, etc.)
    - Is there an independent review of the inspection or the results of the inspection? ☐ Y ☐ N
        - If yes:
            - Identify who
            - Describe extent of independent review
    - Provide inspection information not provided above

Operational Control

- What other operational controls exist to ensure compliance with the law?
- Provide other operational controls—be specific.

STEP II

Identification of Potential Updated/Added Controls

This step is designed to identify *potential* updated or added policies, education/training, and procedures that could be put in place to ensure compliance with the above-stated law. Please answer as clearly and concisely as possible with the goal of identifying suggestions, ideas, updated controls, added controls, etc. that could be implemented to ensure compliance.

Adequate Policy or Procedure

- As the Compliance Partner, in your opinion, if a policy or procedure already exists, is it adequate to ensure compliance with the above-stated law? ☐ Y ☐ N ☐ N/A
- If no:
    - Does the policy or procedure need to be amended?
    - What amendments are necessary?
    - Describe any additional or updated policy or procedure changes that should be considered to enhance compliance.
    - Do you anticipate barriers or obstacles with new policies or procedures? ☐ Y ☐ N
        - If yes:
            - Identify potential barriers or obstacles.

Education/Training Needs

- As the Compliance Partner, in your opinion, should additional or updated education/training be put in place to ensure compliance with the above-stated law? ☐ Y ☐ N ☐ N/A
- If yes:
  - Why should education/training be updated?
  - Describe the purpose or effect of additional training
  - Who should be trained?
  - Should the training be mandatory? ☐ Y ☐ N
  - How should the training be conducted?
    - ☐ Informal (on the job training) ☐ formal or ☐ both
  - How often should the training be conducted? (once, yearly, etc.)
  - How should completion of training be documented?
  - Do you anticipate barriers or obstacles with additional or updated education/training? ☐ Y ☐ N
    - If yes:
      - Identify potential barriers or obstacles.

STEP III

Identification of Concerns or Compliance Risks Not Previously Identified

This step is to identify any *additional* concerns and/or compliance risks that the College needs to be aware of in order to be in compliance with the above-stated law. This step identifies any barriers or obstacles that might exist. This step is *not* to be used to restate any question or answer stated above.

For any concern or risk that is being identified, please keep in mind the following:

- What are the realistic and probable risks (not previously stated above) that the institution is facing and must overcome to achieve the objective of complying with the above-stated law?

- What risks (not previously stated above) "keep you up at night"?
- This is not placement of blame; this is identification of barriers and obstacles that may have prevented the institution from being in compliance with the law in the past, in the present, or in the future.
- Please be clear and concise; identify the context, conditions, and consequences of the risk and noncompliance with the risk.

Risk statements are not limited in number. You should write as many or as few as necessary to identify the noncompliance risks (not previously stated above) that the institution is facing in reference to this specific law.

Concern/Risk Statement

As the Compliance Partner, in my opinion, to be in compliance with this specific law, regulation, or policy, the institution needs to do the following:

ABOUT THE AUTHOR

Judith W. Spain is a Professor Emeritus and an attorney licensed to practice in Pennsylvania, Ohio, and Kentucky. She served as Assistant Dean of the College of Business, MBA Director, and Association to Advance Collegiate Schools of Business (AACSB) Coordinator at Eastern Kentucky University, a large public institution.

Judy also served as General Counsel at Eastern Kentucky University. She conceived and implemented the first compliance program and served as the Chief Ethics and Compliance Officer. Judy was employed as General Counsel and Chief Ethics and Compliance Officer at Manhattanville College, a small private institution, and developed the first compliance initiative. She presently serves as the Compliance Collaborative Program Consultant for the Georgia Independent College Association.

She holds the Certified Compliance & Ethics Professional (CCEP®) designation by the Society of Corporate Compliance and Ethics. Judy is a member of the SCCE Board.

Judy authored *Higher Education Compliance: Blueprint for Success,* the only book designed to assist higher education compliance officers in implementing a compliance program.

She also authored *Compliance Risk Assessments: An Introduction,* published by SCCE.

Judy has an active consulting practice, Higher Education Compliance Consulting. The firm specializes in all higher education compliance issues, ranging from Title IX to lab safety to review of student or employee handbooks. She assists clients in creating compliance programs, provides training on a wide variety of compliance matters, and reviews policies and procedures.

To employ Judy to conduct a compliance assessment, review policies, or provide training, contact her through www.higheredcomplianceconsulting.com

ENDNOTES

1 John F. Kennedy Speech | Rice University

2 United States Sentencing Commission, Guidelines Manual, §8B2.1(b)(2), comment. (n. 1 and 3).

3 United States Sentencing Commission, Guidelines Manual, §8A et. seq.

4 Sentencing Reform Act of 1984, Pub. L. 98-473, S. 1762, 98 Stat. 1976.

5 United States Sentencing Commission, Guidelines Manual, §8A et. seq.

6 United States Sentencing Commission, Guidelines Manual, §8B2.1(b)(2), comment. (n. 1 and 3).

7 https://www.washingtonpost.com/national/2019/06/19/how-did-nasa-put-men-moon-one-harrowing-step-time/?arc404=true

8 United States Sentencing Commission, Guidelines Manual, §8B2(b)(1), comment. (n. 1).

9 https://www.washingtonpost.com/national/2019/06/19/how-did-nasa-put-men-moon-one-harrowing-step-time/?arc404=true

10 A Successful Failure: A Brief History of the Apollo 13 Mission - Bell Museum (umn.edu)

11 Constitution Day and Citizenship Day (ed.gov).

12 John F. Kennedy Speech | Rice University

13 United States Sentencing Commission, Guidelines Manual, §8B2(b)(5)(A) and (B).

14 United States Sentencing Commission, Guidelines Manual, §8B2(b)(5)(C).

15 John F. Kennedy Speech | Rice University

16 United States Sentencing Commission, Guidelines Manual, §8B2

17 United States Sentencing Commission, Guidelines Manual, §8B2(b)(2), comment. (n.1 and 3).

18 United States Sentencing Commission, Guidelines Manual, §8B2.1(b)(4)(A).

19 United States Sentencing Commission, Guidelines Manual, §8B2.1(4)(B).

20 United States Sentencing Commission, Guidelines Manual, §8B2.1(b)(4).

21 United States Sentencing Commission, Guidelines Manual, §8B2.1(5)(c).

22 Family Educational Rights and Privacy Act (FERPA)

23 https://er.jsc.nasa.gov/seh/ricetalk.htm

24 How did NASA put men on the moon? One harrowing step at a time. - The Washington Post

25 USSG sec. 8B2(b)(1) and Application Note 1

26 USSG sec. 8B2.1(b)(2) and Application Notes 1 and 3)

27 USSG sec. 8B2.1(b)(3)

28 USSG sec. 8B2.1(b)(4)

29 USSG sec. 8B2.1(b)(5)

30 USSG sec. 8B.2.1(b)(1)

31 USSG sec. 8B2.1(b)(5)

32 USSG sec. 8B2.1(b)(6)

33 USSG sec. 8B2.1(b)(7)